## About Demos

Demos is a greenhouse for new ideas which can improve the quality of our lives. As an independent think tank, we aim to create an open resource of knowledge and learning that operates beyond traditional party politics.

We connect researchers, thinkers and practitioners to an international network of people changing politics. Our ideas regularly influence government policy, but we also work with companies, NGOs, colleges and professional bodies.

Demos knowledge is organised around five themes, which combine to create new perspectives. The themes are democracy, learning, enterprise, quality of life and global change.

But we also understand that thinking by itself is not enough. Demos has helped to initiate a number of practical projects which are delivering real social benefit through the redesign of public services.

We bring together people from a wide range of backgrounds to cross-fertilise ideas and experience. By working with Demos, our partners develop a sharper insight into the way ideas shape society. For Demos, the process is as important as the final product.

**www.demos.co.uk**

First published in 2004
© Demos
Some rights reserved – see copyright licence for details

ISBN 1 84180 137 2
Typeset by Land & Unwin, Bugbrooke
Printed by HenDI Systems, London

For further information and
subscription details please contact:

Demos
Magdalen House
136 Tooley Street
London SE1 2TU

telephone:  0845 458 5949
email:  hello@demos.co.uk
web:  www.demos.co.uk

# Disorganisation

## Why future organisations must 'loosen up'

Paul Miller
Paul Skidmore

DEM⊙S

# DEM©S

# Contents

# Acknowledgements

Thanks, first and foremost, to Orange for making this project possible. Our particular thanks go to Jayne Hutchinson, Tom Glover, Robert Ainger, Mike Newnham and Alexis Dormandy. At Edelman our thanks to Imogen Bailey, Nicole Harvey, Ben Russell and Olly Scott. At MORI, Andrew Eynon and Nicholas Gilby were always helpful and at NOP World our thanks to Anders Nielsen and Colin Strong.

Throughout the project countless people offered us advice, tips and suggestions and really got involved in the project. Among them were: Elizabeth Coffey, Napier Collyns, Charles Handy, Pat Kane, John Knell, Charles Leadbeater, Andrew Mackenzie, Tony Manwaring, Helen McCarthy, Robin Murray, Kate Oakley, Douglas Rushkoff, Karen Stephenson and Bob Tyrrell. Our thanks to all of them for everything they taught us.

At Demos – that most disorganised of organisations – Tom Bentley, Rachel Briggs, John Craig, Eddie Gibb, Hannah Lownsbrough, Duncan O'Leary and Sophia Parker all helped us to shape the argument. Liam Wren-Lewis and Menaka Nayyar provided brilliant research support. Lisa Linklater saw the report through to production.

As ever though, all errors and omissions remain our own.

Paul Miller
Paul Skidmore
November 2004

# Foreword

You may feel uncomfortable with the idea if you actually run an organisation, but there is a clear message evident from the results of this report: we have to 'let go', or 'disorganise'. Otherwise the employees that we all need, the brightest and the best, will gravitate to more open, more flexible set-ups that fit their values and respond to their aspirations. This will present some real dilemmas.

Ever since Orange was created ten years ago we've talked about a bright future. During those ten years we've helped to change the way people do business. For anyone who spends any time away from the workplace, being without a mobile phone is unimaginable. And we've only just begun.

In the coming ten years mobile voice communications will be just one facet of what Orange offers, and with high-speed wirefree data communications the transformational potential will be even greater. So we have an inherent and vested interest in the way organisations evolve. Accordingly, we want to provoke thought and debate about the way organisations change, the rate at which they can change and the way all of us, not just as employees but as the wider public, are affected by those changes.

We chose to work with Demos because we wanted the widest possible view from an organisation that does not compartmentalise work, but rather sees it as one facet of day-to-day life that feeds to and from wider social, economic and regulatory trends. I'm sure there will be plenty you can relate to. There is much in the report that struck a real chord with me.

But never mind the *next* ten years, one of the things which really hit home was the extent to which business has changed over the *past* ten years. All the time, we are living through a series of small, sometimes barely perceptible developments that collectively have a huge impact. These changes include the emergence of some completely new types of organisation such as the regulators Ofwat, Ofgas, Ofgem and Ofcom. These are completely new entities, with new employees, which have a marked influence on the way many other organisations function.

No matter what sector you are involved in, it seems as if every company has had to become technology dependent. Every organisation is now underpinned by an IT infrastructure. The quality of the infrastructure has an immeasurable impact on a company's effectiveness and the quality of your employees' working lives.

Two-thirds of business leaders say they have started introducing more flexible working conditions for their employees. One of the big enablers is mobile computing and telecommunications, but we all need a real sense of balance and good judgement in the way those solutions are deployed. But is flexible working a good thing?

On the one hand, mobility can contribute to a happier, more motivated workforce. It enables people to spend more time at home; pick the kids up from school more often; avoid wasted, frustrating hours commuting. On the other hand, we could be headed for a backlash. In the UK we work the longest hours in Europe, and the boundaries between work and home life are already merging. Tools for more flexible working hours could be perceived as a means to eek out even longer working hours. So, will people put their foot down and say, 'No, enough is enough'? Certainly, the emergence of more flexible working creates new management demands, requiring new management skills and greater awareness of the consequences.

In the past businesses went their own way. Shareholders could vote with their feet, but other stakeholders just had to put up with it. In recent years shareholders have become ever more interventionist and they have become just one voice among many. Today it is the employees, not their employers, who own the means of production through their intellectual capital, and consequently they wield far more influence. If they walk out of the door, they take an irreplaceable part of the organisation with them.

There is also the wider public and a knowledgeable media. Consumers know more than ever, they care more than ever, and they make their buying decisions accordingly. The media scrutinise companies on every front, investigating, for example, value for money, health and safety, service quality, and the environment and business strategy. Is this simply the start of a trend? Have we reached a point of equilibrium? Or is it, in fact, a cycle?

As you will see, the report possibly raises more questions than it answers. Indeed I know that the central thesis, a gravitational pull towards disorganisation, is a contentious point. However, the idea is to get people thinking and I believe it will succeed in doing exactly that.

As much as anything I think this report emphasises that there is no such thing as a state of organisational equilibrium. Instead, we are going through constant dynamic changes, deeply intertwined with wider changes in society at large. And I for one cannot wait to see what the future will bring.

Mike Newnham
Vice President, Business Solutions, Orange UK
November 2004

# 1. Introduction
## Why organisations matter

*Imagination starts with individuals but flowers in groups, and it needs the power of an organisation to bring it to its full potential.*

Charles Handy[1]

Love them or hate them, organisations are part of all of our lives. We work for them. We buy from them. We depend on them for our security and safety, for the clothes on our back and the money in our pocket. Some of us own or manage them; others inspect, probe and regulate them.

Organisations enable human purposes to be achieved on a large scale. They help us to do the work we could not do alone. We like to think of ourselves as living in a peculiarly individualistic age, in which we have become authors of our own scripts and need no longer defer to the authority of others. At work, rest and play, our lives are characterised by unprecedented opportunities to shape our own lives, from what we consume, to where we go, to whom we befriend. Yet this freedom only makes it more important that organisations are there to enable and co-ordinate all these choices.

That the nation's diet, for example, has become so much more diverse has only been made possible by the emergence of a complex system of production, distribution and supply that connects growers in countries thousands of miles away to the kitchen tables of British consumers. Individualism has made us more, not less, dependent on organisations.

Organisations generate the norms and expectations without which our society could not function. They capture the knowledge, the resources and the trust that we need to reproduce our lives from one day to the next like an effortlessly simple instruction manual. That we wake in the morning to find our world much as we left it the previous day is the result of the organisations that populate our lives.

Organisations embody and communicate our values. Organisations are an expression of the individuals that work for them or consume the goods and services they produce. But they also shape their identities in return. The companies we choose to buy from, the schools we send our children to, the good causes to which we donate time, energy or money, all say something about who we are, and the times in which we live. Particular organisations often become synonymous with particular moments in history: the East India Company, the Ford Motor Company, Coca-Cola, Microsoft, Google. In the modern world, organisations are part of what it means to be human.

Organisational life can be a story of aspiration, altruism and endeavour. The fictional 'Bailey Building and Loan' in Frank Capra's classic movie *It's a Wonderful Life* finds its inspiration in the innumerable real-world organisations that have stirred affection and loyalty from their employees, customers and communities alike. Even in the most adverse conditions, organisations can be the breeding ground for shared values, social cohesion and solidarity. From the sprawl of Detroit to the quaint Utopia of Saltaire (the Victorian industrial village built by philanthropist Sir Titus Salt), and from the glass, steel and marble of the Square Mile to the coalfields of South Wales, organisations can be the foundation of enduring civic identities and alternative visions of social life.

Yet organisations can also be insensitive, frustrating, unresponsive, painful places, where customers are greeted by the cold, impersonal hand of bureaucracy, employees find themselves downsized at a moment's notice, shareholders' wealth is at the mercy of managerial whim and citizens' pension funds are rendered valueless by reckless stewardship. And from the South Sea Company to Enron, some organisations have also come to live in infamy, contributing to misery with acts of neglect or malevolence that would probably be unthinkable for almost any one of the individuals within them.

In short, the kind of organisations we inhabit and interact with exerts a powerful influence on the quality of our lives. How and why those organisations are changing are therefore questions that matter deeply to all of us.

## Hyper-organisation and disorganisation

Over the next decade and beyond, organisations and the people who work within them face two compelling, but countervailing forces for change.

The first is what we call *hyper*-organisation. From Weber to Wal-Mart, the history of organisations has partly been a story about the restless pursuit of greater efficiency. About the search for better, faster and cheaper ways to make money, sell products or win wars. About figuring out how, for a few hours each working day, to order the lives of a group of people in the most rational possible way given the objectives of the organisation as a whole.

Rightly or wrongly, we tend to view the last two decades as a time when the strength of this force has been unusual, if not downright unprecedented. Organisations re-engineered in the eighties, rationalised in the nineties and outsourced in the noughties. Whatever the language, the underlying logic has been the same: how to strip out unnecessary positions, processes, purchases – and people – in order to improve the bottom line, and survive in a competitive environment teeming with new, and increasingly transnational, predators.

The second force is what we call *disorganisation*. Changing expectations of working life place new demands on organisational strategy. Employees want more human organisations with greater autonomy and flexibility. They want an experience of work that is aligned with their values. They want a workplace forged in the image of their identities, not a workplace that tries to define them. They want organisations that can let go, and grant them a greater say in how things are run.

What makes disorganisation compelling is that it is a vision that until recently many could only dream about, but which is now becoming ever more viable at scale. As Thomas Malone writes in *The Future of Work*, 'For the first time in history, technologies allow us to gain the economic benefits of large organisations like economies of scale and knowledge without giving up the human benefits of small ones, like freedom, creativity, motivation and flexibility.'[2]

For those who have survived to tell the tale, flattened hierarchies have brought employees authority and autonomy, once the exclusive preserve of those at the top of the organisational pyramid. Flexible working already releases some employees from the nine-to-five grind. The relentless competition for talent brings higher salaries for those who can command them and the freedom to rewrite the rules of their engagement with the workplace. Technology unleashes new possibilities for organising work in ways that are more aligned with other priorities, from family life to civic duty.

So far though, the benefits of disorganisation are being distributed highly unevenly. A few 'case study companies' have blazed a trail. For every Richard Reed at Innocent Drinks who encourages his people to choose their own job title, and for every Ricardo Semler at Semco who lets employees set their own manager's salary, there are thousands of other leaders who would like to follow suit but would not know where to start. But in truth, most organisations have sought to accommodate hyper-organisation and disorganisation at the same time, sprinkling the elixir of greater autonomy and flexibility among its most valuable human assets while letting their average employee bear the brunt of the competitive winds.

Disorganisation has the force to unravel or explode the closed routines and forms of control upon which organisational security and predictability have traditionally relied. It is important because the traditional virtues of working for organisations are being undermined. We believe an inherent unsustainability is emerging in current patterns of organisation. This is being seen in rising levels of stress, falling levels of job satisfaction and a deep foreboding about the future of working life. At the moment these pressures are being felt mainly by employees, but in time they will be felt by organisations themselves.

This report focuses on how organisations can learn to carve a more sustainable and equitable path between hyper-organisation and disorganisation. Our belief is that organisations and their leaders will need to recall Reinhold Niebuhr's Serenity Prayer in this task, 'God, grant me the serenity to accept the things I cannot change; the courage to change the things I can; and the wisdom to know the difference.'

However, we recognise organisational choices, and those of their leaders, are not theirs alone to make. They are conditioned in part by the ever more competitive and complex environment in which organisations find themselves. None of us are, however, mere pawns in some institutional chess game. Of course, organisational forms are shaped by a complex set of interactions: between historical traditions, future imperatives, and the existing frameworks – civic, legal, regulatory and political – which set the rules of the game, and shape which team wins. But organisational life is not a lottery, no matter how much it may feel like that at times.

By ballot box or boycott, investment or invocation, we have an opportunity to shape the way that organisations work, and the principles and practices on which they are based. No organisation has been granted a licence to operate indefinitely. Most depend on ongoing processes of renewal and legitimacy that we can directly influence, if not control. Recognising that we have this capacity is a crucial first step in understanding the rationale for this project.

### Here and now

Our focus in this report is on the UK where today there are 1,226,915 organisations – and this figures does not include the many people who are sole traders or self-employed.[3] That's around one organisation for every fifty people in the UK. Nearly 1.25 million batches of headed paper and business cards. Nearly 1.25 million tax returns or financial accounts to be filed. Nearly 1.25 million nameplates, business plans and mission statements. The organisations in the UK today fall into three broad classes of organisation: private companies, public sector organisations and non-profit organisations.

The reason for writing this report now is that we believe a unique arrangement of influences has come together to make disorganisation the dominant dynamic of organisational life.

First, there is a reshuffling of the boundaries between public, private and non-profit organisations. Our basic forms of organisation have not changed very much since the nineteenth century. We have relied on the joint stock company, the company limited by guarantee, the chartered institute, the trade union, the charity, the public agency among others as platforms for almost all human activity. But we are entering a new era when the building blocks of organisational life are being repositioned.

Of course, the old legal underpinnings will continue to exist as vehicles for organising different kinds of activity. But their usefulness as institutional signposts of the values that underpin them has declined. The private sector has lost its monopoly on enterprise, the voluntary sector its monopoly on altruism, and the public sector its monopoly on democratic legitimacy.

At the same time the external pressures on organisations are also in a state of flux, prompting new questions for decision-makers within organisations. These are not new pressures – business has always been subject to competition and demands for accountability and always had to make the most of new technologies. The difference is in the ways that the pressures are combining. Departments might need to be downsized at a moment's notice; jobs outsourced and offshored to lower-cost centres thousands of miles away; and new regulations responded to rapidly. Post 9/11, security has also risen up the agenda not just of Western governments but also of companies and charities, organisations that have had to change the way they work as a result.

Another reason is a growing awareness of the negative experience of work for millions of Britons today. What the rising profile of the dark side of organisations tells us is that the desire for disorganisation transcends traditional divisions of high pay, low pay or blue collar/white collar. Stressed executives whose family life suffers as they are unable to leave the office feel the wish for a little more 'elbow room' as much as manual workers repeating the same task day in day out who want a little more autonomy and the facility to develop their own skills and ideas. In short, disorganisation is an issue that almost every organisation will have to face.

## About the report

The first step in understanding how to respond to the desire for disorganisation is to understand its nature and deep-rootedness. We examine changing identities and rising aspirations of employees about what organisations should be capable of. We also show how these changing attitudes are being played out in practice, through demand for flexible working arrangements, changing ideas about the types of organisation people would like to work for and changing attitudes towards leadership. This is the focus of Chapter 2.

We then go on to consider the external pressures on organisations, which often go against the internal pressure for disorganisation and towards hyper-organisation. These are pressures that demand more rigid systems of accountability, more regimentation and greater levels of centralised control. In Chapter 3, we examine how these factors are changing, and the questions they are raising for decision-makers.

In Chapter 4, we offer a possible typology of future organisations to help think through how the tensions outlined in the report might play out in practice. No one organisational model will prevail but our typology indicates ways that organisations can evolve to accommodate their employees' expectations and aspirations. With such a vast terrain to choose from, and on the assumption that the most visible trends should already be filtering into organisational strategy, we have opted to focus our analysis on those types of organisation we think could form an influential part of the institutional landscape in the UK in ten years' time. They may not come to dominate the GDP or labour market statistics, nor do they need to in order to be important. But they will send forth ripples of reform throughout the UK's economic and social life as other organisations adapt to keep pace with new ways of organising for success, attracting and retaining talent and building high-trust relationships.

Finally, in Chapter 5, we offer some conclusions and a set of tough questions that every organisation should be asking itself today if it is to navigate this uncertain future. Consistent with our view that organisational forms are a product both of historical accident and deliberate strategy, this chapter frames the choices, which organisations and the individuals within them will need to overcome, transcend or resolve.

### Methodology

This report stems from a Demos project developed in association with Orange called 'The Future of Organisations'. The project consisted of a number of strands of research:

O   Extensive desk research drawing on a wide range of data sources and academic disciplines.

O   Telephone interviews undertaken in September 2004 by NOP World with 500 senior business decision-makers in the UK to help us understand the pressures that UK business leaders are feeling for organisational change.

O   A series of expert interviews with leading thinkers on organisational change and trends.

O   Face-to-face interviews with 1037 working members of the general public undertaken by MORI in September 2004 to add to our understanding of working life today.

O   A workshop facilitated by Charles Leadbeater with ten leading thinkers and practitioners to help develop our typology of future organisations. This was held at Demos in July 2004.

Both our research and the analysis that flows from it have been skewed towards business organisations, partly because business has been the source of so much organisational innovation in recent decades. But we also recognise that the story of organisational change is about much more than just the private sector, and that businesses themselves are increasingly subject to the actions of non-business organisations, such as regulators, campaigning social movements or even terrorists threatening their premises and personnel. There are signs, too, that publicly managed or mandated organisations, for so long desperate to mimic the most recent (or even not-so-recent) private sector fads and fashions, are now acquiring a renewed confidence in the distinctive 'public value' they help to create.[4]

For businesses, understanding organisations and how they are changing is a crucial imperative. These are their competitors, customers and suppliers. The way that their needs and wants, strengths and weaknesses, adapt over the coming years will be crucial to their fortunes. A clear analysis of what is happening to organisations may not enable them to predict with certainty what will happen, but it will ensure they are better placed to anticipate and respond to change when it happens. For policy-makers, it is essential to recognise that the administrative environment we create is not neutral. It is skewed towards particular organisational models rather than others. The age when government would have tried to 'pick winners' may be gone. But it is still worth understanding the ways in which policy and implementation shape organisational development in the longer term. And for individuals, it is worth suspending your current assumptions about organisational life, and thinking about the kinds of organisations you would like to work for, partner with, buy from or sell to.

If we care about the organisations we are going to have tomorrow, now is the time to be thinking about how we want them to look and feel; what we expect them to do and how we expect them to do it; and the investments, interventions and reforms we need to be making today to give this preferred future the best chance of unfolding. These are issues with which all sectors, organisations and individuals should be engaged.

# 2. Inside Out
## How people power is driving disorganisation

In the summer of 1998 three friends well on the their way to successful careers in marketing, engineering and management consultancy found themselves manning a stall selling fruit smoothies at London's Jazz on the Green festival. On either side of the stall were two bins marked 'yes' and 'no', and across the top a banner which read 'Do you think we should give up our jobs to make these smoothies?' At the end of the day the bottles in the 'yes' bin greatly outnumbered those in the 'no' bin. They walked into work on Monday and resigned, and Innocent Drinks was born.

A jazz festival seems the perfect birthplace for a company that has made improvising around the conventions of organisational life its driving principle. Its workplace culture is defined by informality, with its three founders leading by example by taking the job titles 'Boss Hog', 'Chief Squeezer' and 'Top Banana'. The workspace abounds with bean bags, table football and baby photos. A personal touch to people management goes far beyond a strict first-name terms policy to include experience days such as a bungee-jumping excursion for employees reaching certain performance targets; a scholarships scheme to enable employees to fulfil a personal charitable or educational goal; a £2000 'baby bonus'; and an extra five days holiday for newly-weds. This commitment to values and human scale are embedded in corporate ethics, with a high proportion of profits donated to charity and the establishment of the Innocent Foundation to support NGOs worldwide.

Innocent is a company that is very serious about play. Customers are invited to call the company to have a chat or suggest recipe ideas on its 'banana phone', and to drop by the HQ at Fruit Towers in West London to say hello or take a tour. Friday beers, cheese and wine evenings and company picnics litter a packed social calendar, the highlight of which is probably the free annual two-day Fruitstock festival the company puts on in London's Regents Park as a tribute to its origins.

But its playfulness also extends to its subversion of traditional ideas about hierarchy, with great emphasis placed on giving all employees the freedom to innovate and use their initiative. Maintaining the small-business feel as the company expands is an article of faith for co-founder Richard Reed: 'You see a very direct link between your efforts and your output, which is incredibly rewarding; you feel genuinely proud of what you make and of seeing staff deliver after they are given responsibility.'

The company's record speaks for the success of this approach. From 1998 to 2003, just one employee left the company. Since then, the organisation has snagged 30% of the £70m smoothie market, won the National Business Awards for People Development in 2002, been finalists for the 2003 Outstanding People Development award, and won the 2004 Employer of the Year award.

Innocent's success seems to turn the principle that nice guys finish last on its head: 'In business, we are ruthlessly nice,' says Reed. 'We are a pretty naïve bunch of people, employing people like us – people who would never work for a tobacco company – and that just keeps working in our favour.' But it also shows that for companies that can master the art of disorganisation, the rewards – material and emotional – can be very impressive.

In this chapter, we show why Innocent is not an isolated experience, but simply one expression of a more widespread cultural shift occurring to a greater or lesser degree across many organisations in the UK. To understand what this shift means for organisations, we need to understand both its underlying logic and the various ways in which this is beginning to find concrete expression in organisational structures, cultures and practices.

We focus on three areas:

○ individualism and identity
○ flexibility and human scale
○ leadership and participation.

## Individualism and identity

Nowadays, we take it for granted that we live in a more individualistic society than we did 50 years ago. The Dunkirk spirit of collective endeavour, sacrifice and solidarity has given way to much more footloose and fragmented identities.

Affluence and the expansion of educational opportunity have weakened although not dispelled the impact of social class on life chances and professional pathways. Large-scale post-war immigration has created a greatly more diverse society, simultaneously both solidifying some ethnic identities and diluting others. A great social and political movement has helped transform the lives of women by challenging the expectations projected on to their lives by earlier social conventions. Compared to their grandmothers, women today have far more opportunities to participate fully in education, work and community; no longer are their lives simply defined by a responsibility for household and family life. At the beginning of the twentieth century, around five million women worked, making up 29% of the total workforce. By 2000 the figure had risen to 13 million, representing 46% of the total workforce.[5] Women's membership of community associations more than doubled between 1959 and 1990, rising by 127% compared to just 7% growth for men.[6] Expectations about personal lifestyle choices, from marriage and family life to sexual orientation, have become much less pronounced.

Ideas of 'career' are shifting too. *The Office* sitcom manager David Brent sums up the way things worked in the twentieth century better than most, 'You grow up, you work half a century, you get a golden handshake, you rest a couple of years and you're dead.' In the twenty-first century this will no longer be the case. Demographic change is destabilising traditional notions of identity in relation to career structure, so that people increasingly have a number of 'mini-careers' retraining and reskilling throughout their working lives.

All of this has had a dramatic impact on organisations. Wholesale shifts in the structure of the economy and the labour market have disrupted many traditional affiliations to class, vocation or community. Between 1950 and 2000, the proportion of the working population employed in distribution and services more than doubled, and now accounts for 70% of the workforce. Manufacturing, by contrast, now provides only 16% of employment compared to nearly 40% in 1950.[7] Where once people might have defined themselves through working in the mines or shipyards, trade union membership or participation in associated community organisations, the rise of a service-based economy has afforded far fewer sources of common identity.

The growth of individualism has been accompanied by the rise of a set of 'post-materialist' values[8] as people move beyond what Charles Handy, in a reference to a traditional African expression, describes as the lesser hunger for the things that sustain life towards the greater hunger for an answer to the question 'why?'[9]

Pat Kane writes about 'players' who are more interested in a 'play ethic' than a work ethic:

> *This is 'play' as the great philosophers understood it: the experience of being an active, creative and fully autonomous person. The play ethic is about having the confidence to be spontaneous, creative and empathetic across every area of your life – in relationships, in the community, in your cultural life, as well as paid employment. It's about placing yourself, your passions and enthusiasms at the centre of your world.*[10]

At its most extreme this is embodied in highly paid, highly educated citizens of nowhere but everywhere – people variously known as 'post-modern professionals', 'global nomads', or what Robert Reich calls the 'symbolic analysts'.[11] Richard Florida has documented the rise of a creative class whose skills in knowledge-based, high value-added industries are accompanied by a taste for vibrant, bohemian and diverse social and cultural environments, with a great competitive advantage accruing to the cities able to offer them.[12]

In our conversations with organisational leaders we heard on several occasions that they believe people are increasingly making choices about which organisation to work for not just on the basis of the pay packet but also for its values, ethics and the sense of meaning the job might offer. We were told that in graduate recruitment interviews the questions that now often come back from the interviewee is as likely to be 'What is your policy on climate change?' as 'How much will I start on?'

In our NOP survey, over the next five to ten years, 48% of business leaders expected employees to increasingly ask to be involved in corporate social responsibility (CSR) activities such as improving the environmental impact of the business, volunteering in the community or corporate charitable giving. The demand was expected to be higher in large companies – in companies with over 500 employees, 76% thought it was likely that employees would ask to be involved.

What these shifts in identity indicate is that organisations will need to adapt to a greater extent to the values of their employees in order to retain talent. They will need to give them greater choice in the way that they work and greater ability to personalise their experience of work.

### Flexibility and human scale

If 'play' is becoming a defining value of how work should feel, 'craft' is perhaps emerging as the value upon which it should be structured. This is the case both literally and figuratively. Literally, in that one of the hallmarks of disorganisation is a yearning for the human scale that accompanied pre-industrial age patterns of working life; and figuratively, in that it symbolises the desire for individuals to craft their work in more flexible ways that are supportive of other commitments to family or community.

The latent desire for work and organisations more compatible with 'craft' is a backlash against the complexity, speed and pressure of modern working life. Fed up with work swamping any chance of work–life balance, employees opt for more life, less work in a decisive way. Whether it is the string of books and TV shows that follow working families giving up on the rat-race, the emergence of 'slow food' or the word 'downshifting' entering the popular lexicon, we want our experience of life to be authentic, not just in the sense of the word as the opposite of superficial, but in the sense of the etymological roots it shares with the word 'author'; we want to be authors of our own lives. But our organisations have yet to adapt, seeming big and impersonal compared to our ideal of working life.

In our MORI poll of the general public we found nearly one in five employees in the private sector would like to work for a smaller organisation. Perhaps this is a symbol of the desire for smaller, more human scale places to work. A quarter of workers in the public sector feel this. The desire to work for smaller organisations is concentrated in the AB social grouping where 27% would rather work for a smaller organisation rather than in the C2 or DE groupings where 17% and 14% would like to work for smaller organisations respectively. It also seems more men than women (15% compared to 10%) would like to work for larger organisations.

The age group where the desire to work for smaller organisations is strongest is among 45–54-year-olds where 25% across all sectors would like to work for smaller organisations. This is the generation at the leading edge of the shift away from the traditional twentieth-century career structure.

Desire to work for 'human scale' organisations may also have something to do with the level of management of employees. When we asked our NOP sample of business leaders whether they would like to work for a smaller or larger organisation, 71% said smaller compared to only 7% who would like to work for a larger one.

### Case study: WL Gore

WL Gore is a company that makes waterproof jackets. It also makes parts for satellites and cardio-surgery and is a world leader in the dental floss market. In 2002 its sales reached $1.4 billion. But perhaps most impressive of all is that it has done this with no managers, secretaries or employees.

Instead, it has a global network of 6000 associates, which own the company between them. There is no strict management hierarchy – leaders arise naturally, but only when others agree to follow. All associates have one to three 'sponsors', performing different roles – helping a new associate get started on the job, advocating that the associate gets credit and recognition, and making sure the associate is fairly paid. Salaries are decided by 'compensation committees', with members of an associate's team scoring their performance over the year. All in all, these mechanisms make the company appear very different from standard multinational manufacturers.

But this so-called 'lattice' method of organisation, claims founder Bill Gore, is 'underlying the facade of authoritarian hierarchy' in every company. His plan was to expose the process by which he felt the real work gets done. 'Most of us delight in going around the formal procedures,' he says, 'and doing things the easy way.' Or, as one Gore employee puts it, 'Why go to someone with a title when you can go to someone with an answer?' The lack of traditional structures help to create an atmosphere of freedom, one of WL Gore's key mantras. 'Freedom is the source of innovation, invention, trying new things, and bringing about change and new projects,' preaches Gore. 'It is crucial to the long-term success of an enterprise.'

Key to the notion of freedom is that teams organise themselves. But Gore noticed that as a plant became large, this simply stopped being possible. 'This begins to happen somewhere in the range of 150–200 people,' he reckons. 'At about this number you begin to hear conversations change from *we* decided, we did, or we planned, to *they* decided, *they* told us. That is the signal that the organisation is not together.' So WL Gore now has a policy whereby its plants are only built to hold about 150 people. As the workforce naturally expands it starts to get uncomfortable, and when a group reaches over 200 it is split into two. 'From an accounting point of view this breaking up is always a stupid thing to do,' concedes Gore, '[and] a team of 150 can't afford certain resources that in high-tech operations you need.' To solve this problem, they use factory clustering, where as many as a dozen separate plants are located within a 10-mile radius. Gore has no doubt that any difficulty is worth it: 'I suppose there are high capital investment enterprises where it just isn't feasible to do this. It's too bad, because it is a waste of the human resource to fail to do this.'

These teams are encouraged to get to know one another. Individual emails and memos are discouraged, with the philosophy being that it's better to go and talk to the person face to face. It's very clear that this small team style makes it a great place to work – recently WL Gore was voted top in '*The Sunday Times* 100 Best Companies to Work For'. In it 86% of staff said they believe they can make a difference at the company – 85% 'just love working for Gore'. It seems no coincidence that the self-organising team structure has produced both an enjoyable working atmosphere and economic prosperity. For Gore, it is undoubtedly the key: 'Our success, our very survival, depends on having created a society, a family, of teams.'

'Craft' – in the sense of flexibility and designing our organisations around individual needs – is being driven in large part by equality movements. Foremost is the changing role of women in the workplace. Make no mistake, the glass ceiling is intact: women make up only 23% of the senior echelons of the civil service, only 9% of senior positions in British businesses and are still paid 19% less than their male counterparts in the UK.[13] But as women make up a larger proportion of the workforce, fewer and fewer traditionally male dominated sectors and organisations can remain in the diversity dark ages.

Helen Wilkinson has termed this the 'genderquake' and says that as women have entered the workforce there have been implications for the way organisations are structured:

> *Organizationally . . . business is becoming more feminine. And it's not just the talk about family-friendly companies, flexible scheduling, or mentoring, all of which are targeted at female workers. Rigid hierarchies of control are giving way to management styles that combine tough control over some functions with much looser, more team-based approaches.*[14]

The trend is set to continue as more and more organisations realise the benefits of gender diversity. As Wilkinson says:

> *More and more, success at work depends on traditional feminine attributes, like flexibility and dexterity. Today's work-place values team-based networking and interpersonal skills. Skills that historically have been necessary to thrive in the private sphere – skills like conflict resolution, communications, and juggling – have suddenly acquired a premium in the public sphere. And as women have moved into the labour force, from the private to the public sphere, they've taken these skills with them.*[15]

The next diversity quake could come from the disability movement.[16] There are over ten million disabled people in the UK, one million of whom would like to work but are currently unemployed – the so-called 'missing million'.[17] The Government and disability movement are attempting to change this. The final sections of the Disability Discrimination Act came into force in October 2004, which means that all employers must make 'reasonable adjustments' to ensure their workplaces are accessible to disabled people. On the surface, this could be interpreted as just providing ramps up to the entrances of office blocks. But more enlightened employers are realising the benefits of offering personalised solutions for disabled employees, giving them flexibility as to where, when and how they work.

In our survey of UK business leaders, a majority (59%) thought flexible working (such as varying working hours, the ability to work from home or being able to take unpaid leave for personal reasons) would become more prevalent in their organisations in the future. In large companies with over 250 employees, over 80% said they had introduced flexible working already and intend to extend the arrangements in future.

Their reasons for introducing flexible working seem clear: 85% say that flexible working increases job satisfaction, with an even larger percentage agreeing in large companies. There are conditions though – 97% agreed with the statement that flexible working requires trust between organisation and employee.

When we asked business leaders how many workers they thought would ask for more flexible working in the future, they suggested that they thought one in four workers would be likely to increasingly demand it. In those companies that already offer flexible working, leaders thought demand would be even greater (32% demand within those companies who are using flexible working against 16% demand within those who do not), suggesting that once it has been tried, the benefits of flexible working are obvious and thus demand increases.

It seems that demand for flexible working lags behind the perceived benefits: while 81% think that flexible employment benefits both the company and its employees and 59% said they were likely to introduce flexible working in the future only 51% expect actual demand from employees to rise.

Technology is also playing an important role in enabling us to craft our own experience of work. The history of organisation is in part a history of competing ways of arranging and sequencing sets of tasks in the most efficient, effective or profitable way. Just as Ford's perfection of the assembly line enabled it to outperform its competitors in the first half of the twentieth century, so Toyota's system of continuous improvement and just-in-time production enabled it to keep costs and inventory levels down and profits up in the 1980s.

Today, advances in technology, communication and manufacturing mean that the traditional barriers between demand and supply, between consumer and producer, are themselves being broken down. Mass production is giving way to mass customisation, with consumers themselves participating in the production of goods and services. Leading PC manufacturer Dell offers its customers 16 million possible configurations and does not begin to assemble a machine until it has detailed instructions from each individual customer.

This technologically enabled flexibility and customisation can also increasingly be applied to employees. Technology is enabling collaboration and co-ordination to be achieved at a distance, no matter whether employees are at home, in the office or on the move. In our survey of business leaders, 91% of those questioned believed that new technologies would be important drivers of organisational change over the coming years. The vast majority of them (88%) saw technology as an opportunity rather than a threat. Of the sample, 60% agreed the workplace of the future would involve less face-to-face interaction.

## Leadership and participation

The third expression of disorganisation is a loosening of traditional configurations of power and authority, including changing ideas and practices surrounding leadership.

Frederick Taylor's principles of 'scientific management' – decomposing processes into their constituent parts, removing or redesigning parts that do not add value and putting the organisation back together again – dominated understanding of industrial processes for much of the last century. Then in the 1970s and 1980s, 'management' gave way to 'leadership', reflecting a change from a bureaucratic emphasis on doing things better to a new emphasis on doing better things. This in turn reflected the growing realisation that organisations of every stripe exist in an uncertain and unstable operating environment. This requires senior personnel who have the vision to anticipate or even precipitate changing currents, to help their organisations adapt, and to refresh and retell their organisational narratives and stories in light of changing circumstances.

This emphasis on leadership over management, particularly in Anglo-Saxon economies, has been one reason for the growing 'cult of the chief executive officer' (CEO), with senior executives receiving vast remuneration on the basis of some (questionable) assumptions about the relationship between executive talent and corporate performance. Fortunately the days when 'leadership' meant developing faster and more efficient ways of firing people are gone. This was embodied in (often American) business leaders such as 'Chainsaw' Al Dunlap, who once posed on a magazine cover wielding a machine gun to show his take-no-prisoners attitude to leadership, or Jack Welch, who built GE into one of the world's most successful companies using the principle of firing the 10% of his managers who performed least well each year.

But as Joel Bakan, author of *The Corporation*, puts it, 'These men now seem like barbarians, uncouth and uncool, as ridiculous as their red suspenders. Today's leading CEOs cultivate compassion and seem genuinely concerned about how their corporations' actions affect social and environmental interests, not just their stockholders.'[18] So the cult of the CEO has not gone away, but it has learned that ruthlessness is not a characteristic that either employees, or for that matter shareholders, always value.

But how is leadership changing now? When we asked our sample of business leaders to predict where future CEOs of UK companies would come from, 60% of them thought they would come from outside the UK, of which 31% of them thought they would come from Europe, 16% from Asia and 13% from North America, compared to 40% who thought they would come from the UK.

In our survey, 61% of business leaders thought that senior positions in their companies were currently more likely to be held by older rather than younger people. However, 45% of these people thought this was likely to change within the next five to ten years, so that younger people increasingly take up senior positions. Moreover, 33% of business leaders expect their organisations to become less hierarchical in the coming two years as opposed to only 25% who thought they would become more hierarchical. If our sample is to be believed, leaders will become younger, more diverse in terms of their background and will have to be more able to operate in less hierarchical settings.

Some commentators suggest they may even have to be able to operate in organisation democracies. The 'hyper-organised' way of taking decisions was to make them centrally and impose them locally. But could hierarchy break down altogether? Could organisations, particularly businesses, change their governance so that employees, rather than managers, decide? On one level this is about leaving decisions to front-line staff and not interfering in operational decisions, but at its most extreme this might mean employees voting on strategic decisions such as the pay of senior managers. We're quite used to business organisations being subject to shareholder democracy through votes on major decisions and at annual general meetings, but will they increasingly be subject to employee democracy?

The benefits for businesses of democracy have been extolled by Lynda Gratton in her book *The Democratic Enterprise*[19] and even further by MIT professor Thomas Malone, who sees a revolution brewing in the way employees are involved in setting the strategy of their employers in his book *The Future of Work*.

> *We are at the early stages of . . . a revolution in business – that may ultimately be as profound as the democratic revolution in government . . . Once again, the result will be a world in which people have more freedom. A world in which power and control in business are spread more widely than our industrial-age ancestors would have ever thought possible. A world in which more and more people are at the centre of their own organisations.*[20]

In this environment, social networks will become an increasingly important way of understanding and operating within organisations. While no longitudinal data exists to show how connected people are within their own organisations, our MORI questionnaire showed inequalities in the number of people that different social groups know on first name terms in their organisations. One group that stands out are 35–44-year-olds, where 22% of them claim to know over 100 people on first name terms in the organisation they work for. This is more than double the proportion of working 15–24-year-olds who claim to know the same number and also double the proportion of working 55-plus-year-olds who claim to know over 100 people. So just working for longer is no guarantee of having stronger social networks at work.

The question all this raises is that if the case for disorganisation is so compelling, what holds organisations back? It is to this question that we now turn.

# 3. The Bends
## Why external pressures hold disorganisation back

In the late 1860s the city of New York began construction of the Brooklyn Bridge. Submerged in special construction capsules called 'caissons' sunk deep in the riverbed of the Hudson for hours on end, workers quickly began to complain of muscular pain and cramped joints, as well as disorientation, headaches and dizziness. In 1880, French physician Paul Bert noticed that the symptoms of 'caisson disease' – or what workers had dubbed 'the bends' because of its effect on their limbs – were identical to those experienced by deep-sea divers.

His insight paved the way for a new understanding of the effect of major changes in pressure on the internal biochemistry of the human body. Overly rapid decompression, caused when someone submerged underwater ascended to the surface too quickly, was responsible for a range of physiological complaints. In the most serious cases, when bubbles of air formed in the blood (similar to the moment when a bottle of fizzy drink is opened) the effects could be fatal. Divers the world over are now taught to decompress in stages to give their bodies time to adjust to the changes in pressure.

To understand why the logic of disorganisation has not yet been embraced more fully, we need to recognise that many organisations today face their own version of 'the bends'. Confronted with the massive pressure exerted on them by their external environment, most find it a difficult enough struggle to maintain their internal coherence as it is and view such radical changes in their internal cultures and values systems as profoundly risky.

Here we focus on three important external pressures:

O    intensifying competition, both from home and abroad;
O    the growing demand for accountability, which often manifests itself in new regulation and legislation;
O    growing concerns about global security, which put into question the responsibility of organisations for the safety of their employees.

If disorganisation is to be sustainable, the pressure from within – from employees – needs constantly to be balanced against these external pressures. If it is not balanced properly, the implications will rebound eventually on the organisation's performance, but first they will affect the welfare of employees.

During the 1990s, while the pressures for disorganisation were growing, so were signs of employees having even less autonomy and control over their working lives. This was a period in which job satisfaction steadily declined. In the British Household Panel Study (BHPS), when asked the question: 'All things considered, how satisfied or dissatisfied are you with your present job overall?' the average score fell steadily from 1991 to 2002. And numerous other surveys show the percentage of employees who are 'very satisfied' with their jobs falling over the same period.[21]

As Professor Francis Green of the University of Kent says of working life in 2004:

*People feel that they have to work harder – not just longer hours, but more intensively. They feel they are on the go all day and that contributes to more stress. And they are recording that they have less control over their daily tasks. There are more targets, more rules, less trust.*[22]

According to Madeleine Bunting it is the working culture of many organisations in the UK that is sick. In her book *Willing Slaves* she points to statistics showing British full-time employees work the longest hours in Europe (an average of 43.6 hours a week compared to a European average of 40.3) and that those figures are rising. Between 1998 and 2003 the British average went up 0.7 hours. Bunting blames this on what she calls our 'Overwork Culture' which is particularly prevalent among 30–39-year-olds where a fifth of workers are working over 60 hours each week.[23]

Robert Taylor who led the Economic and Social Research Council's (ESRC) *Future of Work* Programme – a comprehensive review of working life in the UK undertaken in 2002 – also paints a bleak picture:

> *Today's world of work is much less satisfying to employees than the one they were experiencing ten years ago. It has also grown more stressful for all categories of employees without exception – from senior managers to manual workers. Most people say they are working much harder in intensity and clocking on for more hours of work than in the recent past. They may not be so discontented with their lot that they are in the mood for outbursts of militancy but it would be the height of complacency to ignore or underestimate the central message that suggests a marked decline has taken place in levels of worker satisfaction.*[24]

Another ailment of modern organisational life is a feeling of disconnection between employees and their superiors. Our own research with MORI suggests nearly one in five (18%) people working in large organisations in the UK say they never have a conversation with their boss's boss. Nearly a quarter of people (23%) say they have a conversation with their boss's boss less than once a year. This points to the exclusion of a significant group of UK employees from having any chance of influencing the future of the organisations they work for.

And to see how deep dissatisfaction goes you only have to take a look at cultural reference points. The 1990s was the decade of *Dilbert*. More recently, of course, there's *The Office*, Ricky Gervais and Stephen Merchant's comic masterpiece set in the fictional Slough regional office of Wernham Hogg paper products. It's funny, sure, but it is also deeply unsettling for the majority of managers in the UK who cringe as they see in it elements of themselves. It has become a cultural embodiment of what we feel about working life at the beginning of the twenty-first century.

So it seems that, at the moment, the external pressures on organisations are being felt more strongly than the pressure from within. This chapter considers each of the three external pressures in turn, presenting evidence about how they are viewed by organisational decision-makers. The overall results of our NOP survey regarding the importance of drivers of organisational change and how strongly they are seen as being a threat are shown in Table 1 and Table 2 respectively.

### Table 1

| Drivers ranked as 'very important' | Percentage |
|---|---|
| Regulation and legislation | 74% |
| Changing customer demands | 67% |
| New technologies | 60% |
| New members of staff | 45% |
| Competition from the UK | 42% |
| Competition internationally | 21% |
| New management theory | 16% |

### Table 2

| Drivers seen as threat | Percentage |
|---|---|
| Competition from the UK | 55% |
| Competition internationally | 45% |
| Regulation and legislation | 35% |
| Changing customer demands | 8% |
| New management theory | 4% |
| New members of staff | 3% |
| New technologies | 2% |

## Intensifying competition

Competitiveness is the major preoccupation of most UK businesses and business organisations. The past half-century in particular, has seen UK businesses subjected to the harsh winds of international competition as globalisation has marched on. Writing about those who use the word pejoratively, *Financial Times* columnist John Kay writes 'Once, privatisation was used as an umbrella term by opponents of market-oriented reforms. Today, globalisation has a similar interpretation. Globalisation is things that people hostile to the modern market economy dislike.'[25] But for former World Trade Organization (WTO) adviser and *Economist* journalist Philippe Legrain:

> *Globalisation has the potential to do immense good. Just look at the amazing leap in American and European living standards since the Second World War... Study after study confirms it: freer trade makes us richer. Foreign competition keeps companies on their toes; new technologies spread faster; countries specialise in what they do best and buy the rest for less from abroad.*[26]

But as markets have become open to competition and monopolies broken down, global competition has had immediate and negative impacts on people within organisations. Corporate restructuring, downsizing, delayering, outsourcing, offshoring are all tools for finding the extra competitive advantage in a global market place and they can all put the future of particular employees into uncertainty.

In our survey of business leaders we asked whether national and international competition are seen as important drivers of organisational change. For the moment at least, competition from the UK is seen as being most important: 42% saw it as being very important, while 38% saw it as being somewhat important. This compares to 21% seeing competition internationally as a very important driver of organisational change and 21% seeing it as somewhat important. When asked, 55% of those questioned saw competition from the UK as being a threat while 45% saw competition internationally as being a threat.

The trend towards offshoring has perhaps been the most high profile manifestation of intensifying competition in the UK media recently. But our survey of business leaders showed 29% thought that this trend was likely to increase over the next decade while 71% thought it would not. This suggests either the importance placed on offshoring by the media is overstated or that UK business leaders are unprepared for its implications. Given the speed of globalisation and the rapidly growing educated middle class in countries such as India and China, we believe the evidence points to the latter.

Part of competing against other organisations is competing to keep up with consumer desires and trends. In our survey of business leaders, 67% thought changing consumer demands would be a 'very important' driver of organisational change while 28% saw it as a 'somewhat important' driver of change. And 81% of them saw these changing demands as an opportunity rather than something neutral or a threat.

In their book *The Support Economy* Shoshana Zubhoff and James Maxmin argue that in our complex bewildering world it will be the organisations that provide 'deep support' that will thrive.[27] But does 'deep support' for the customer come at the price of 'deep support' for the employee? It is here that the role of trade unions comes into question. Madeleine Bunting writes of work in the 1990s, 'instead of joining a trade union people sought private solutions, treating themselves to aromatherapy or a nice holiday in the sun instead.' But she is worried about the space that has been left: 'The undermining of the unions has left a vacuum in Britain. Who speaks for the working man and woman? Where is the campaign to wrest back control of our time, to demand the right to a day's work which leaves one with the energy to do more than stagger home and slump on the sofa?'[28]

## Regulation and legislation

The relationship between private enterprise and government is often envisioned as verging on the allergic. In truth, it is a story of deep and historic interdependence. Companies have always depended on regulation and legislation to create the kind of operating conditions, legitimacy and trust needed to sustain private transactions. Governments, for their part, are dependent on companies for the economic growth on which tax revenues and public spending depends. In this sense, for example, limited liability status is a kind of compact between firms and government.[29]

Despite growing discomfort at excessive corporate power and influence, this interdependence continues to this day. In *The Risk Management of Everything*, LSE Professor Michael Power argues that organisations are being 'turned inside-out'.[30] Internal systems, controls and governance models that would once have been strictly the organisation's private concern have increasingly become objects of public scrutiny and regulation because of the collective consequences if they prove defective. High profile corporate failures such as BCCI, Polly Peck, Barings, Equitable Life and Enron have had a hugely negative impact on share prices, public trust and the financial fortunes of customers and employees.

But turning organisations inside out leaves fewer and fewer areas of organisational life not subject to some kind of scrutiny. A common reaction is for organisations – and their leaders – to try to take a greater level of control over every area of activity that they can. This can come at the expense of individual employees who feel they are being overly monitored and disempowered by centralised control. It has been accelerated by a greater focus on the individuals at the top who will be responsible for failure if it takes place. One example is the financial services sector, where the regulator has introduced a system of 'named individuals' within large financial services firms who could go to jail if regulations are breached.

It is also extenuated by the fear on the part of some companies of what has come to be known as a 'compensation culture' as people come to expect that if something goes wrong somebody should pay and take the blame. This is not limited to consumers who feel they have been wronged, but also includes employees. As Robert Taylor found in the ESRC study, 'There is clear evidence of an increase in the amount of litigation coming from employees that is being experienced by managers in their workplaces.'[31] In the 2002 study, 16% of managers said that their companies had had to spend more money on legal advice over employment issues over the past three years compared with only 6% who said they had spent less and 67% about the same.

When we asked business leaders to rate the importance of regulation and legislation as a cause of organisational change over the next decade, 74% rated it 'very important' and 22% as 'somewhat important'. While not heavily ranked as a threat, it is seen as being the most important single driver of organisational change.

## Craving security

In many large companies, security has assumed a much greater profile than at any time in recent history. In a 2003 survey of International Security Management Association (ISMA) members (who are drawn from Global 200 and Fortune 500 companies) there was overwhelming consensus that business continuity and personnel safety have been propelled to the top of the risk management agenda.[32] Senior executives we spoke to told us that the effect that concern about security is having on choices made around UK boardrooms about organisational structures and procedures should not be underestimated.

The rise in importance of security is usually explained with reference to 9/11; in a survey carried out by Janusian of individuals responsible for corporate security in companies in Britain, two-thirds of respondents had seen their budgets rise since 9/11.[33]

There is also the fact that the penalties for organisations getting security wrong are so much greater. With the introduction of the crime of corporate manslaughter and the growing trend towards personal accountability, board directors could find themselves personally liable when something goes wrong. The rise of litigation is particularly important in corporate terms because it brings not only the risk of direct financial loss, but also reputational damage, the consequences of which can last for years.

For Nassim Taleb, mathematician, trader and author, security is related to the ability to handle and understand 'black swan' events:

*A black swan is an outlier, an event that lies beyond the realm of normal expectations. Most people expect all swans to be white because that's what their experience tells them; a black swan is by definition a surprise. Nevertheless, people tend to concoct explanations for them after the fact, which makes them appear more predictable, and less random, than they are. Our minds are designed to retain, for efficient storage, past information that fits into a compressed narrative. This distortion, called the hindsight bias, prevents us from adequately learning from the past.*[34]

Even if no breach of security occurs, organisations are increasingly subject to damage because of the potential of a break of security. Be it comedy terrorists at Windsor Castle, hunt protesters making it onto the floor of the chamber of the House of Commons or newspaper reporters finding security loopholes in baggage checks at airports, the culture of security is affecting many organisations. Security drives organisational change by exerting a pressure for centralised control in an unpredictable world. This affects disorganisation because of the trade-offs it can often entail between security and predictability and the privacy and freedom of employees.

Historically, a 'perimeter fence' approach to security has been adopted by many companies where they make themselves secure by keeping people out. A small group of 'security professionals' decide who has access to what and when. These security departments are often made up of people with armed forces or security service backgrounds, well used to a command-and-control approach.

But for employees this can lead to a feeling of being constantly watched. Security can get in the way of doing their jobs in the ways that they feel is best; becoming something that is only ever seen when it is being obstructive. And given the importance of security, employees often feel they have no recourse or ability to question and adapt policy or practice. Security becomes something that is 'done to' employees rather than something they have a stake in. And when approached like this, security policy can breed suspicion between colleagues, and between employees and decision-makers about motives. For example, swipe card gates that are meant to keep out unwanted visitors can be seen as an instrument of control over working hours, checking who is in the office and when.

But as Rachel Briggs has written, it does not have to be like this. A new agenda for 'commitment-based security' is emerging over which employees take greater control and responsibility for security, which then becomes positively embedded in the culture of organisations.[35]

The relationships between these three types of pressure are multifaceted and often unpredictable. The changes they will bring about are not simple to understand – there will rarely be a direct relationship between cause and effect and unintended consequences will abound. But each of these pressures *can* be managed in such a way that organisations steer a sustainable course away from hyper-organisation and burnt-out, stressed employees.

In Chapter 5 we will return to how we believe organisations can achieve this and the dilemmas they will need to resolve between the desire for disorganisation and the need for survival in a seemingly ever more hostile environment. First, though, we describe practically how disorganisation can be manifested in new types of organisations emerging over the coming decade.

# 4. Darwin's Appendix
## A typology of future organisations

As Charles Darwin, the father of modern biology, sat, quill in hand, penning the final touches to his *Origin of Species*, he no doubt marvelled at the advantages evolution had gifted him over other beasts. But the beauty of his theory was not just that it explained the many things he found useful about his body, like opposable thumbs or a hyper-developed cerebral cortex, but also the continued existence of some things he found much less helpful. Like his appendix.

Darwin's appendix offers us an insight into some of the most puzzling paradoxes of organisational life. For as we look at organisations, we see some models and methods of co-ordination that appear inherently superior to any alternative we might think of, as if they were natural laws of organisation, institutional truths we take to be self-evident. Yet we also see routines, ways of working or whole entities that, to put it politely, would not be part of our plans if we were starting from scratch. Few who spend time interacting with or within an organisation have not at some point been confronted with the odd, the inefficient or the downright infuriating, only to be told 'it's just the way things are done around here.' And although organisations often view their external environment as threatening, uncertain and ever-changing, the experience of people inside organisations is often of remarkable, occasionally very frustrating, stability. Old habits can die thumpingly hard.

With this evolutionary metaphor in mind, the purpose of this chapter is to propose a typology of organisational forms that could be much more influential in 10 years' time than they are now because of disorganisation. The typology consists of the following:

○    public value company
○    plug and play organisation
○    democratic firm
○    navigator organisation
○    faith-based company
○    open-source financier
○    new union
○    live/work organisation
○    icon organisation
○    auction army.

One or two may be clearly recognisable, reflecting the capacity of some organisational forms to adapt to considerable changes in their environment while preserving a set of core characteristics. Others may be hybrids, fusing elements of more familiar organisational types to produce something distinctively new. Still others may be radically new, reflecting the potential for periods of relative stability to be punctuated by periods of rapid change, in which conditions emerge for whole new organisational forms to emerge. Where examples exist today we have included them as short case studies to help illustrate the typology. For each type we will look at the response to change, typical employees, culture and ethos, and size.

## The public value company

It would be unwise to predict the downfall of any of the current legal models of organisational form due to disorganisation. The limited company, the charity and the public sector organisation will continue to exist as vehicles for organising different kinds of activity. But their usefulness as institutional signposts of the values that underpin them is in long-term decline. Selling off public utilities such as gas, telecommunications and electricity, and encouraging different sectors to play a role in the provision of public services such as social care, have blurred the boundaries between public, private and community.

Until recently, however, the assumption has been that unleashing market disciplines on public institutions was the best way to create economic value (primarily through efficiency gains and lower costs to the taxpayer). The rise of public value companies, by contrast, is based on the application of public values to private institutions. These values may still include lower costs, but they also include other things that people value when it comes to the provision of certain kinds of goods: sustainability, fairness, legitimacy and so on.[36]

So-called 'public interest companies' are one example of what this might look like, operating within frameworks set by policy-makers but at arm's length from government and accountable more directly to their users and communities rather than capital markets. Currently, there are a few examples in the UK including housing associations, Glas Cymru (the Welsh water utility) and Hackney Learning Trust. In addition, proposals for 'community interest companies' are aimed at providing a new legal shell for the social enterprises, which are an increasingly important part of the local social fabric.

The definition and structures of public value companies will no doubt diversify and morph as organisations play with different configurations of public, private and community boundaries, and as the values and expectations of consumers and citizens catch up to this changing reality.

○ **Reaction to change**: blurring of boundaries between old legal models.
○ **Typical employees**: values-driven, high-achievers, frustrated by previous experience of other sectors.
○ **Culture and ethos**: public-spirited but entrepreneurial.
○ **Size**: diverse, although likely to be smaller than conventional public sector organisations in order to remain nimble.

## The plug and play organisation

An expansion in the number of smaller organisations and freelance individuals could lead to new organisations to support them, and to provide functions such as administration, human resources or the regulatory interface that would be prohibitively costly or difficult for any one small organisation to provide itself. These companies would create value by allowing individuals to 'borrow' economies of scale for particular things.

Plug and play companies would themselves be a driver of organisational diversity by making sustainable forms of organisation, and particularly micro-organisation, that otherwise might not be logistically or financially feasible.

Since they could drive down the cost of administration for whatever service they perform, these may become not-for-profit companies with directors drawn from the small organisations or individuals that use them. One example of this approach is the 'Mezzanine' cluster model operated by the Community Action Network (CAN), where groups of not-for-profit organisations come together to share office spaces and facilities, driving down their fixed costs by pooling overheads. Each organisation has a seat on the board of the company set up to administer the facility.

- o  **Reaction to change**: growth of freelancers, micro-businesses and small non-profit companies.
- o  **Typical employees**: experienced, functional experts, well-connected and entrepreneurial.
- o  **Culture and ethos**: highly specialised; emphasis on building high-trust relationships with customers.
- o  **Size**: would tend to be fairly small, although some may grow.

## Case study: The Mezzanine

The last thing small not-for-profit organisations want to have to spend their very limited resources on is entering into the legal, bureaucratic and practical problems of office management. But having a well-managed, well-located office is essential for such organisations to be effective. Community Action Network, an organisation aiming 'to stimulate new, entrepreneurial ways to tackle social problems more effectively and more efficiently' came up with a solution.

'We began with five tenants and a short lease on 3500 square feet just off Leicester Square,' explains Adele Blakebrough, the co-founder and Executive Director of CAN. 'Our aim was to network social entrepreneurs within the voluntary sector: to increase their profile, to raise their sights and to help them learn from each other.' Now, they help run the Mezzanine in Waterloo, with 25 tenants in over 19,000 square feet of space.

Though CAN partly administrate the project, Mezzanine Services Ltd is an independent company limited by guarantee, with its own full-time office manager. Each organisation in the office is a member of MSL, paying a monthly fee to pay for the operating costs, including office equipment, mail and franking services, and a communications and IT infrastructure that would not be out of place in a multinational business.

The economies of scale and sharing these facilities mean the Mezzanine saves its members a total of £230,000 a year in direct costs. But for Blakebrough, this is only part of the benefits the members receive. 'I am convinced that for the social sector there is a huge benefit to be had if organisations can get together to share knowledge.' The environment – full of bright young social entrepreneurs – is ideal for 'cross-fertilization'. As well as sharing resources the tenants share networks and ideas, developing cross-sector themes and opening up doors for new projects.

But such integration and co-operation between members is not left up to chance. New tenants are asked to put on a lunch or drinks event to explain who they are and what they do. The Mezzanine has its very own 'animator', a job that consists of nurturing the relationships between organisations, and encouraging collaboration. 'The Mezzanine model offers voluntary organisations a real opportunity to apply entrepreneurial approaches to their work,' praises Matthew Thomson, Director of Development at TimeBank, a member of the Mezzanine.

Though the Mezzanine has encountered its fair share of difficulties ('If you give people really nice coffee,' Blakebrough notes,' they will drink loads of it!'), the future looks bright. In 2004 it moved into a bigger, brighter office in London Bridge, incorporating a next generation of entrepreneurs. With lots of interest from other people wanting to set up similar 'platform' offices, CAN have even developed their own consultancy – Cluster Consulting. Soon, perhaps, small not-for-profit organisations having to put up with low-quality facilities and back-street offices may be a thing of the past.

## The democratic firm

As we discussed in Chapter 2, one manifestation of disorganisation is giving employees a greater say in the future of the organisations they work for. At the moment democratic principles seem at odds with the structures of most current organisations. But are they necessarily incompatible? A handful of 'case study companies' have shown that the answer is not necessarily. Ricardo Semler's Semco in Brazil has pioneered highly distributed and transparent models of decision-making. Film-makers the Farrelly brothers encourage everyone on set, from the actors to the grips, to make suggestions how any aspect of the movie could be improved. And evidence suggests that, given the right conditions, large groups of diverse individuals are much better at predicting the future than small groups (for example boards). Within ten years we could see many more examples of corporate strategy be decided through the ballot box.

○   **Reaction to change**: Changing work ethic and people wanting a say in the running of the organisations they work for.
○   **Typical employees**: people for whom work is more than a job.
○   **Culture and ethos**: high employee satisfaction, strong emphasis on flexible working, meritocratic but fair.
○   **Size**: medium to large.

---

### Semco

When Ricardo Semler inherited the helm of the family firm in 1980 he inherited a wealth of problems, including near bankruptcy, vast inefficiencies, low productivity and poor morale among employees. A four-year flurry of expansion and product line extension did nothing to boost the flagging spirit of the company, however, largely due to the bureaucratic and slow processes embedded in the organisation's structure. So Semler called a general meeting of employees, giving birth to a more democratic, humanistic system that took inspiration from his previous experience of playing in a rock band. Though initially there was a negative reaction to the company's transition from a top-down system to one based on democracy, ethics and egalitarianism, the shift has paid off. As Semler says, 'We took a moribund company and made it thrive, chiefly by refusing to squander our greatest asset, people'

Ten years later Semco had grown by over 900% and risen up the Brazilian industrial rankings from fifty-sixth to fourth place. All of this has been achieved without a slogan or mission statement. Rather, Semco is guided by open dialogues, collaboration, participation, teamwork, transparency and a radical power shift whereby employees vote for major decisions that affect the company as a whole. Employees are treated like free-willed adults, and are given no set working hours, no dress code, no office or desk assignments, no perks based on rank, no secretaries or receptionists, no set amounts of holiday time, and so on. The guideline is to use common sense and to maintain high productivity. This involves employees justifying their own position every six months, rotating jobs, and other practices designed to promote discussion, expansion, and very strong employee-company relationships and involvement.

## The navigator organisation

A complex world confronts citizens and consumers with a bewildering array of choices about how to live their lives. In response, they will increasingly turn to organisations that help them to navigate this terrain by offering what Maxmin and Zuboff call 'deep support'. These organisations will succeed not by making products or delivering services (although they may help to customise them to individual needs) but by developing highly personal, long-standing and trusting relationships with their clients. They will become *the* one organisation that a customer turns to for all of their household transactions, from finding a plumber to buying a car to opening a bank account. They will also focus not just on getting the best deal but satisfying ethical concerns and other demands that consumers may have. They will be highly dependent on the quality of their relationships with both suppliers of the goods and services that their customers want, and with the customers themselves. As such, they will need to develop new and different ways of defining and improving quality, valuing relationships and rewarding the frontline staff that build them.

- O  **Reaction to change**: ever-increasing choice and complexity for consumers.
- O  **Typical employees**: back-office team expert with excellent supply chain management, relationship building and

negotiation; frontline managers able to build and sustain high-trust relationships.

○   **Culture and ethos**: high trust; versatile.

○   **Size**: some will seek trust through high visibility and size; others will reflect their 'human scale' through a smaller size.

**The faith-based company**

The flipside to the rise of individualism within employees is that, once we have it, we can be flummoxed by choice. The choices extended to us as individuals seem to grow exponentially. Both as consumers and employees the number of potential organisations we can have relationships with is growing. This adds to the complexity of every choice we have to make, but what does that mean for the shape and culture of the organisations servicing those choices? Kevin Kelly sees one possible way for each of us to simplify the choices we make:

*When you have a zillion different options, you have to have different ways of cutting through. One of the ways you cut through those options is you use value sets. You have a set of values that enable you to navigate, because it automatically says, 'Don't bother with these choices. You don't have to worry about these.'*[37]

People increasingly say that they want to make purchasing decisions in line with their beliefs and values. While mainstream brands and retailers may attempt to cater for these (supermarkets selling Halal meat for example), they fall down on their overall performance since they also provide products and services that some people will disagree with. Our prediction is that companies catering to specific religious groups are likely to increase in influence. They will try either to be become vertically integrated (managing everything from point of production to point of sale) or new companies will spring up over time making sure that the entire product and value chain is in line with the values of a particular religious group. Mecca Cola is perhaps the most prominent example of this so far. The rise of faith-based brands brings with it the possibility for a fusion of organisational mission and ethical or spiritual principles. This is analogous to the Congregationalist capitalism of the nineteenth century, when men such as Sir Titus Salt provided excellent social amenities for their workers in return for sobriety, religious observance and hard work.

○ **Reaction to change**: backlash against increasing choice, people wanting to put their values into purchasing decisions and their everyday working lives.
○ **Typical employees**: people who do not believe in a separation of values in life and values at work, people who practise what they preach.
○ **Culture and ethos**: values based, with organisational culture mirroring that of the customers they serve.
○ **Size**: medium or large – need economies of scale to be viable.

### Case study: Islamic Bank of Britain

The 1.8 million strong Muslim community in Britain has long had a dilemma when it comes to banking. Under Sharia (Islamic law) money itself has no intrinsic value, and the giving and receiving of interest, known as 'riba', is forbidden. Hence accounts on services that use interest in some way – practically all deposit accounts and mortgages, for example – are theoretically out of bounds. While some Muslims have decided to use conventional banks in the past, few have done so happily.

The newly opened Islamic Bank of Britain hopes to solve this dilemma. At its head is managing director Michael Hanlon, who has been working hard with the Financial Services Authority (FSA) to work round the problems of riba. Together they have managed to design an almost complete product range. Instead of mortgage loans, for example, the bank buys a house and sells it to a would-be home-owner at a premium using fixed monthly instalments. Creating deposit accounts has been tricky because the FSA demands that banks guarantee to return a depositor's capital. But the settled upon solution is that savers waive any guarantee, and the money is then pooled and used to buy goods, which are sold for a profit. This profit is then split between the bank and the depositor.

This is not the first time such products have been available in the UK. HSBC, for example, having recognised the potential of this market, already offers Sharia-compliant pensions, home loan schemes and stockbroking services. But these have only had limited success. The Islamic Bank of Britain hopes its greater understanding of the Muslim community and Islamic beliefs will give it the winning edge. Not only are all its products structured in a Sharia-compliant way, but all operations are overseen by a select panel of Islamic scholars. As a result, the bank does not invest in products such as tobacco, pornography or arms.

It is this wider ethical commitment that Hanlon, himself a Christian, hopes will tempt even non-Muslim customers to its products: 'I am not going to play the religious card. We are positioning this as a new bank with an alternative proposition. We want to go out there and compete head-to-head with everyone else. It is fair and transparent. You see more and more people demanding just these values from their banks, so there is a wider appeal to ethically minded non-Muslims.'

There are, inevitably, some doubters. 'What is being proposed with Islamic banking is actually a hardening of the religion,' worries Charles Moore, writer for the *Daily Telegraph*. 'Once there are Islamic financial institutions, how long will it be before Muslims ... seek to establish their own law within [Muslim] areas, the germ of a state within a state?' But Hanlon dismisses such conservative thinking. 'Times have changed. There was no political will before ... but now the government here is strongly promoting greater inclusiveness within society. The tragic events of September 11 changed the world in a lot of ways.'

Islamic banking had previously been considered a niche product, but Hanlon is ambitious, and the sheer size of the market suggests there is serious potential. Recently, the German state of Saxony-Anhalt raised 100 million Euros (£66 million) by issuing the first European 'sukuk', an Islamic bond. If Hanlon succeeds in his further plans to create branches in Europe, where there are at least 15 million Muslims, then this may be the beginning of a new wave of Islamic banking in the West.

## The open source financier

Open source is all the rage. With Linux and Apache now more than just thorns in the side of the big boys of the software world, established players such as Sun and IBM are seeing the value of investing in open source. The basic idea is to provide a methodology for collaborating on the development of products and then sharing the use of the (hopefully better) products that result from that collaboration.

At the moment this is done without any legal underpinning, governed largely according to a set of shared norms and values (such as those held by pioneers of the Internet) that might loosely be referred to as the 'hacker ethic'.[38] But as organisations rather than individuals have a stake in the product, and as open source approaches move further away from their origins in software programming, a new way of formalising the process may emerge. Not withstanding the increasingly commercial business model of open source delivered by IBM, Red Hat or Novell, the resulting model may be something that resembles a new model mutual, which is owned by its members through their investment (albeit perhaps of intellectual as opposed to financial capital), but with the necessary legal protections or obligations required for it to operate in a range of different institutional settings and among a variety of other types of organisation.

○   **Reaction to change**: technology allowing mass
     collaboration in the development of products.
○   **Typical employees**: venture capitalists with a conscience.
○   **Culture and ethos**: based on open source principles and
     the hacker ethic.
○   **Size**: medium.

*Case study: The Open Source Application Foundation (OSAF)*
Mitch Kapor, developer of Lotus 1-2-3 – a 'killer application' that
changed the world of computing – has been one of the big names
in software development for a long time. By 2001 he had served
time as a designer, CEO, entrepreneur, angel investor, activist and,
lastly, as a rather unsatisfied venture capitalist. 'As I sat amidst the
ruins of the dot com world contemplating what to do,' he muses, 'I
was looking for a next thing that would be both personally
meaningful and contribute something to the world of computing.'

The result was the Open Source Application Foundation, a non-
profit organisation with a mission to 'create and gain wide
adoption of Open Source application software of uncompromising
quality'. The product it aims to create, Chandler, has been touted as
a rival to Microsoft Outlook – much to the annoyance of Kapor: 'We
aren't targeting Exchange or Outlook in any direct kind of way, but
inventing a new product. Anybody that actually wants to compete
…will need to go multiple stages down the road.'

The vision is of a fundamentally different Personal Information
Manager, built from basic foundations with the source code kept
entirely open throughout. According to Kapor, in these hard times
for software start-ups the Open Source style of development is the
only way to develop innovative applications. And though OSAF
itself is non-profit making, he would be very happy for others to
make money from their work in the future. The licence scheme will
permit both non-commercial and commercial development on the
code base, with funds being channelled back into further
development.

But the road so far has not been entirely smooth. 'I had some nervousness,' he admits, 'that if you give up too much control too soon then people will take it in directions that you don't want to see it going'. The team of about 15 employees – and Kapor himself – came mainly from traditional styles of programming, many working for Apple or Microsoft, and at times dealing with the external Open Source community has been difficult. An outside critique of the organisation in May 2003 found 'staff lack clarity about the relationship between paid staff and volunteers.'

To deal with this, Mitchell Baker, a long-time Open-Sourcer and Chief Lizard Wrangler at mozilla.org, was brought in to guide OSAF's relations with its growing community. Her role has been to 'help OSAF develop a work style that allows the entire community to participate to the maximum extent feasible'. Now things are looking better: 'The project isn't quite such a fragile seedling, and we are more able to engage.' Gradually, the open source community is learning how to work successfully with OSAF's more rigid structure.

As for funding such ambitiously innovative organisations, Kapor concedes: 'No sane VC would or should fund a venture to compete with the Microsoft monopoly'. OSAF itself was given a $5 million start-up from Kapor, but this is not their only source of funding – impressed with the work so far, the Andrew Mellon Foundation and a consortium of universities gave another $2.75 million to extend the project into use within higher education.

You don't need to encourage programmers to write open-source software; they're already encouraged, since they essentially invented open source for their own amusement. What I would like to see over time is more investment – not for-profit investment, but investment from foundations and the public sector, where a big open-source project would be a public benefit held in the public trust. Having the funding to get stuff started is an area in which I hope that my example will encourage other people.

OSAF's success has, for example, already helped Mitchell Baker further her own ambitions outside the organisation. In 2003 Mozilla Foundation, a public benefit corporation working on open source Internet and email tools, secured $2 million string-free from America Online. If Kapor's belief that 'most good software hasn't been invented yet' holds, then this sort of not-for-profit organisation may be the future of software innovation.

## The new union

Struggling in many places to renew their image and role for a changed world, trade unions could carve a strategically crucial niche for themselves at the interface between our identities as workers and as consumers. As these identities increasingly seem to be in conflict, the ability to navigate the trade-offs could be highly prized. We might see trade unions working with consumer groups, perhaps even merging and then providing services to companies that help them turn a zero-sum game between the interests of employees and the interests of customers into a solution that is in the best interests of all.

O  **Reaction to change**: rising stress in the workplace, increasing working hours, demands for flexible working.
O  **Typical employees**: trade unionists, campaigners, communicators.
O  **Culture and ethos**: versatile, media savvy.
O  **Size**: small to medium, they probably will not rely on mass membership.

## The live/work organisation

For the people for whom work and play are becoming indistin-guishable (Richard Florida calls them the 'creative class') we may see a rise in organisations that not only provide workspace but also offer living space as a response to the idea of creativity coming from close collaboration. Traditionally this has been the artists' collective or the band who live together but as property prices rise it's an idea that might spread. Already some cities are experimenting with ways of encouraging creative professionals through schemes such as 'Creative Lofts' in Huddersfield, which provides live/work space. Of course the concept of mixing work and life to such an extent might be some people's idea of hell.

○    **Reaction to change**: rise of individualism, changing work ethic.
○    **Typical employees:** creatives, players.
○    **Culture and ethos**: unrelenting.
○    **Size**: small.

## The icon organisation

The Beckhams might seem to be just a brand but beneath the surface an organisation with staff, turnover and a market value exists. Relying on a quasi-religious following, the organisation is highly skilled at communication and creating relationships with individual followers. They are also adept at the reinvention of icons and symbols. This celebrity brand, with its accompanying entourage and organisation, shows no sign of waning.

Take Gordon Brown's baby bond idea one step further and consider not just family or government investment in the future of an individual child (from parents, godparents etc.) but investment by private shareholders. What would happen if shares in a child's future were public listed and traded? Just as David Bowie issued 'Bowie bonds' against the value of his future royalties, what if families started issuing bonds against the future earning potential of their children? What sources of information and transparency would be needed to make this work? Would they ever be compatible with ethical principles and privacy?

○    **Reaction to change:** rising individualism.
○    **Typical employees**: ambitious individuals.

○ **Culture and ethos**: competitive, every person for him or herself.
○ **Size**: micro.

## The auction army

Auction sites such as eBay allow cheap auctions of listed products. Imagine if people listed themselves on eBay describing their skills, experience and contacts and their time could be bought and sold and combined to form an organisation or complete a certain project. What means of verifying knowledge would be needed to make this work? How could we build trust and confidence in them?

○ **Reaction to change**: the long wave of technology and growing use of reputation systems.
○ **Typical employees**: today's temps.
○ **Culture and ethos**: a job is a job.
○ **Size**: most suited to small and medium organisations where recruitment costs would normally be more significant.

We want to emphasise that our intention has not been to quantify or rank the importance of these types against each other or against the organisational models we have today. Neither is this typology meant to be exhaustive. Rather, we think it is useful for two reasons.

First, each reflects one possible outcome of the interaction between a set of drivers that are real and present. The types themselves simply help to think through and make concrete the implications of some of these drivers. Thinking imaginatively about the organisations we might have enables us to see how disorganisation might manifest itself in our own organisations. That, we contend, is a valuable process for anyone involved in organisations, because even if these types remain unrealised or peripheral, the drivers they reflect will be having an impact. Conventional organisations may come to reflect or embody in microcosm some of the organising principles we have sought to isolate.

Second, the organisations we *will* have is partly a function of the organisations we *have* had – structures are 'path dependent'. But it also depends on how conducive the conditions are for new organisations to take shape, and these are not beyond our capacity to shape and influence, if not control.

# 5. The Pile or the Man

## Creating new patterns of participation in organisations

On 30 January 1912, Frederick Winslow Taylor sat in a committee room in the United States House of Representatives in Washington D.C. as a panel of hostile interrogators fired question after question at him, determined to uncover the truth behind what the whole country was now calling 'the Taylor system.'

The catchily-named 'Special Committee to Investigate the Taylor and Other Systems of Shop Management' had been convened a year earlier after a strike by workers at the government arsenal in Watertown, Massachusetts. At the centre of the dispute had been the introduction of new management methods based on the principles of efficiency, which Taylor been developing for the previous two decades and which had now earned him considerable fame – and notoriety.

Taylor, founder of the 'scientific management' school and the man responsible for what Peter Drucker called 'the most powerful as well as the most lasting contribution America has made to western thought since the Federalist papers,' had begun his career as a patternmaker's apprentice. But he had risen rapidly up the managerial ladder, thanks to his pioneering approach to achieving efficiency in time and effort through the careful observation and reorganisation of the most minute details of working practices. In the process, he laid down a blueprint for modern organisation that is being followed to this day.

After many hours fending off questions about the impact of his methods on the working man and eulogising about the gains to be had from adopting them, Taylor found himself in the middle of a lengthy peroration on the science of shovelling. If a man was shovelling coal, he explained, he needed a different size and shape shovel than if he was shovelling gravel. Otherwise he would not achieve the regulation 21.5lb shovelfuls which, Taylor had meticulously calculated, gave him the largest pile of material at the end of the day.

Having listened intently to this account, John Q. Tilson, one of the three congressmen on the panel, fixed Taylor with a withering stare. 'You have told us about the effect on the pile,' said Tilson. 'But what about the effect on the man?'

## People first

In this report, we have argued that the same questions – about how to organise ourselves to achieve common purposes while respecting the other things that matter to us as people – are being asked a century later. The pressure to make organisations more productive must be balanced with the desire for them to be more human. In the longer run, the ability of organisations to keep producing innovation and improvement in the way they work depends on their ability to attract, retain and generate commitment among workers and customers with a much wider range of priorities.

The offer that organisations have traditionally made to their employees – of security, shelter and incremental progression in pay and position – is increasingly difficult to sustain, at least beyond a narrow group of core staff. As the external environment facing organisations has become more ruthless and unpredictable, most have sought to retain agility by reducing their costs and liabilities and externalising risk. Employees have been moved off the payroll into part-time or short-term contracts. Support services have been outsourced to specialists to enable a tighter focus on core competences. The decline of trade unions has increased managerial leverage over pay and conditions, with a growing chasm between those in secure, predictable patterns of employment and those locked out. Performance management systems have evolved ever more sophisticated ways of counting and measuring activity and punishing or rewarding the workers that contribute to it.

But many people yearn for a different kind of experience of organisational life – one that affords them more autonomy from layers of managerial oversight, and more freedom to craft their engagement with the workplace in ways that reflect the other things that matter to them. When economic exchange places a growing premium on knowledge and skills that are locked in people's heads, when many of the things that matter most to organisational performance cannot easily be measured, when 'soft' skills have a more obvious link to 'hard' profits, the dilemma facing organisational leaders becomes clear. How can we secure ongoing commitment from our employees when survival in a fast-changing, fragmented world seems to depend on staying nimble and minimising liabilities?

Organisations in the UK do not yet have the answer to this dilemma. In our research we came across startling evidence of just how far organisational commitment goes for UK employees. When we asked whether they thought they were more likely to get a higher salary and greater responsibility with their current employer or by getting a new job with another organisation, two in five (41%) working members of the general public said with another organisation. This applied as much to employees of public sector organisations as those in the private sector.

The expectation of loyalty to an existing employer, and of progression over time within one organisation, seems to have diminished. This may be a realistic assessment of what to expect from today's labour market, but it has important implications. On one hand, organisations must keep learning new ways to motivate and retain staff and help them improve their own effectiveness. On the other, in a world of looser, more flexible relationships between workers and hirers, customers and suppliers, organisations need new ways to communicate with networks of people without trying to bind them into exclusive or hierarchical relationships.

At first sight, what we have called disorganisation seems to add to the pressure. People's growing desire for flexibility drives and encourages organisational fragmentation. But disorganisation is more important than that; the disparate forces it embodies appear to offer the most compelling responses to this dilemma. While Taylorism put the 'pile' before the 'man', the logic of disorganisation is that work can, and should, be built around people – not the other way round.

This organisational logic often can only be found by careful study of the internal rhythms and the external relationships that different organisations embody, what is sometimes called the 'hidden wiring', though organisational logic is more social than electrical. But the fact that it is half-hidden makes it no less powerful, both for the success of organisations and for the conditions and opportunities that it creates for people.

Rather than in their formal leadership structure or their legal constitution, future templates for organisations will emerge from the cumulative interactions of their workers with the formal elements of their structure and operation, such as information technology and accounting. The logic of disorganisation could create new combinations of flexibility and reliability, of human scale contact combined with widespread reach and accessibility, of shared commitment to pooling risks and pressures in return for a greater sense of involvement and creativity at work.

Just how far-reaching that logic proves to be is hard to predict, in part because it depends on choices which are ours still to make about how best to innovate, improvise or ignore our way through the transition. Yet for people in organisations, whatever their station or status, it will be difficult to feel a sense of agency without first answering some of these questions:

○   Where are the opportunities to shape this future?
○   Who will wield them?
○   What are the constraints on widening involvement in decision-making?
○   Who are the winners and losers from disorganisation going to be?

○ What are the elements of a successful organisational strategy for coping with disorganisation?
○ What kinds of learning and knowledge-collection will help organisations to adapt?
○ What role might regulation and public policy play in creating the environment in which new organisational forms develop?
○ How do we foster a longer-term discussion of the kinds of organisations we want and the conditions under which they might emerge?

## Seeing the whole puzzle

Disorganisation will manifest itself in myriad, hybrid ways. Case study companies offer us a glimpse of what prioritising different elements of it – informality, flexible working, devolving autonomy to the frontline, inclusive decision-making, open membership, integration through shared technology, asserting the primacy of values – can look like in practice. Our typology sought to extend some of that thinking to its logical conclusion. But for each organisation the pressures will be felt differently; consequently, how they seek to accommodate them will vary.

One reason why disorganisation will not be automatically embraced is that its benefits will not be distributed evenly or fairly. There will be winners and losers, within and between firms, industries and nations, some of whom may be surprising. In New Zealand, for example, groups of casual workers who are employed picking fruit in areas such as Hawke's Bay already use mobile phones to gain leverage over employers. They text each other the wage that different growers are offering per basket that day before going en masse to work for whomever is paying best and leaving other growers in the lurch. But generally speaking, the distribution will follow familiar patterns with the burden being borne by particular groups of workers and their communities.

As such, disorganisation could help make a decisive shift in the political debate away from the relatively recent concern with the amount of work available towards a renewed interest in the *quality* of working lives. Just as questions were once asked about wealthy factory owners benefiting from child labour, so it must be asked: are the benefits of disorganisation experienced by one group achieved at the expense of the happiness of others?

Those who best answer the questions above will first have realised that disorganisation can be viewed as threatening or liberating, depending on how much, and which parts, of the puzzle of organisational change you can see. The view from the top, looking down, may be very different from the view at the bottom, looking up.

The task for organisational leaders is to make the whole puzzle more visible and therefore less threatening; to find new ways of surfacing and combining the views and aspirations of as many people within their organisations as possible. We believe this implies an approach to experimenting, at least on the margins, with new ways of involving people in decision-making.

It will mean creating new ways of structuring mass involvement in deciding and measuring organisational progress. From the point of view of individual employees these forms of engagement will be different from what has gone before because they will be personal agreements rather than standardised and collective ones.

The organisations that succeed will be those that create more opportunities than they close down. They will mobilise people, individually and collectively, to find responses to the challenges of organisational life that disorganisation presents.

To manage the unpredictability of disorganisation will require that organisations develop new sources of certainty. The best jazz musicians appear to improvise effortlessly, yet their ability is founded on dedication and practice, and their playing takes place within clear harmonic structures and rhythms. In the same vein, organisations may only be able to disorganise successfully in some areas if they can organise more effectively in others. For example, developing systems of communication that are more sophisticated in mapping knowledge and skills across an organisation, providing employees with the means to locate and retrieve this information more simply, could make flexible working more feasible, as it would reduce the need to locate people physically in the same spaces at the same time.

Arguably the most compelling area for developing this principle is what Henry Chesbrough of the Harvard Business School has termed the shift to 'open innovation'. The old paradigm – of closed innovation – was based on the view that successful innovation requires control. It assumed that firms must be self-reliant 'because one cannot be sure of the quality, availability and capability of others' ideas: "If you want something done right, you've got to do it yourself." Open innovation, on the other hand, implies that organisations adopt a radically different approach for combining external and internal ideas into new architectures, systems and roles. Open source organizations such as Linux appear to succeed through such disorganisation – enrolling thousands of disparate individuals in the stewardship and improvement of a product simply by appealing to their moral purpose and creative instinct. But they actually also depend on making some things more rather than less concrete: the criteria for judging success, for example, and simple rules for taking part in discussion or development of pieces of the system.

There will surely be limits to how much meaningful participation is possible. One important source of variation will be sectoral. Will participation be confined to knowledge-intensive, high-value added industries where human and social capital are the key ingredients of success, and people the organisation's key asset? Will disorganisation in horticulture look anything like disorganisation in software programming?

How different organisations interpret and respond to these pressures will partly reflect their values in a world in which sectoral status, ownership structure and mission statements are patchy guides to the organisational values that stand behind them.

In past decades, the process of making values real in organisations was often most visible in the handling of conflicts between workers and management, or, more benignly, through decisions about the recipients of corporate charitable giving. But those days are largely gone. Companies are now going through a painful process of realising that they need fuller and more convincing ways of determining and expressing their values. If mission statements and CSR policies fail to have authenticity and practical application, the effects are all too obvious: companies are punished by NGOs, pilloried by a sceptical and cynical media or find themselves with an unmotivated, uncommitted workforce.

So organisations are having to live out their values in the way that they work. In other words, their approach to organisation and disorganisation in practice, creates a cumulative impact which is the most reliable guide to values.

Disorganisation could create new recipes for securing commitment from people, in turn giving them greater autonomy and freedom to make their own personal values real within their working life and their organisations.

The design and development of organisations will have a fundamental impact on the well-being of millions of us over the next decade. It will help to establish whether work, family and personal lives can be combined in sustainable ways. It will influence the distribution of opportunity and wealth in a capitalist economy. It will shape the extent to which economic life can tap the creativity and commitment distributed across communities, and make ingenuity a collective phenomenon rather than an individual trait. This report has argued that our current landscape offers a wide range of paths for organisational evolution, and therefore opportunities for shaping the future.

The question is: are we ready for what we might see?

# Notes

1   Handy in the foreword to 'The New Enterprise Culture', *Demos Quarterly* (London: Demos, 1999).
2   T Malone, *The Future of Work* (Cambridge MA: MIT Press, 2003).
3   Figures (published August 2004) are the most recently available government figures from the Government's Small Business Service Analytical Unit, which each year publishes estimates of the number of organisations in the UK, the people working for them and the turnover of enterprises across all sectors. This excludes self-employed people, organisations without any employees, and all those organisations that don't have a legal status such as certain clubs and societies.
4   See M Moore, *Creating Public Value* (Cambridge MA: Harvard University Press 1997). BBC Charter Review, *Building Public Value*.
5   Office of National Statistics, *A century of labour market change: 1900 to 2000*, http://www.statistics.gov.uk/articles/labour_market_trends/ century_labour_market_change_mar2003.pdf
6   P Hall, 'Social Capital in Britain', *British Journal of Political Science*, Vol 29 Part 3 July 1999.
7   D Greenaway, R Upward and P Wright, 'Sectoral Transformation and Labour Market Flows', paper prepared for the International Economic Association conference on 'Globalisation and Labour Markets', University of Nottingham, July 2000.
    http://www.nottingham.ac.uk/economics/leverhulme/conferences/iea/guw.pdf
8   R Inglehart, 'Globalization and Postmodern Values', *The Washington Quarterly*, Winter 2000, Volume 23, Number 1.
9   C Handy, *The Hungry Spirit* (London: Hutchinson, 1997).
10  P Kane, 'Play for Today' in *The Observer*, see also his book P Kane, *The Play Ethic: a manifesto for a new way of living* (London: Macmillan, 2004).
11  R Reich, *The Future of Success* (London: Heinemann, 2001).
12  R Florida, *The Rise of the Creative Class: and how it's transforming work, leisure, community and everyday life* (New York: Basic Books, 2002).

13    See H McCarthy, 'Girlfriends in High Places' (London: Demos, 2004) and
      *Labour Market Trends*, vol 110, no 12.
14    K Hammonds, 'Work and Life - Helen Wilkinson', *Fast Company*, Issue 30
      December 1999, p. 188.
15    ibid.
16    See P Miller, S Parker and S Gillinson, *Disablism: how to tackle the last prejudice*
      (London: Demos, 2004).
17    K Stanley and S Regan, *The Missing Million: supporting disabled people into
      work* (London: IPPR, 2003).
18    J Bakan, *The Corporation: the pathological pursuit of profit and power* (London:
      Constable, 2004).
19    L Gratton, *The Democratic Enterprise: liberating your business with freedom,
      flexibility and commitment* (London: FT Prentice Hall, 2004).
20    T Malone, *The Future of Work*, op. cit.
21    F Green and N Tsitsianis, *Can the Changing Nature of Jobs Account for National
      Trends in Job Satisfaction?* UKC Discussion Papers in Economics, 2004, 04/06.
22    Quoted in *The Guardian*, 30 October 2004.
23    M Bunting, *Willing Slaves: why the overwork culture is ruling our lives* (London:
      Harper Collins, 2004).
24    R Taylor, *Britain's World of Work – myths and realities* (Swindon: ESRC, 2002).
25    J Kay, *The Truth About Markets: their genius, their limits, their folly* (London:
      Penguin Allen Lane, 2003).
26    P Legrain, *Open World: the truth about globalisation* (London: Abacus, 2002).
27    S Zubhoff and J Maxmin, *The Support Economy: why corporations are failing
      individuals and the next episode of capitalism* (London: Penguin Allen Lane,
      2003).
28    M Bunting, *Willing Slaves*, op. cit.
29    See P Skidmore, P Miller and J Chapman, *The Long Game: how regulators and
      companies can both win* (London: Demos, 2003).
30    M Power, *The Risk Management of Everything* (London: Demos, 2004).
31    R Taylor, *Britain's World of Work*, op. cit.
32    Quoted in *Securing the Knowledge Enterprise, Globally* (Armor Group, 2001).
33    Survey carried out by Janusian Security Risk Management, the results of which
      were presented at a conference on 1 April 2003.
34    N Taleb, 'Learning to Expect the Unexpected' in *The New York Times*, 8 April
      2004.
35    See R Briggs, 'Hidden Assets: putting people at the heart of security' (2004),
      paper available from http://www.demos.co.uk
36    For a more detailed discussion of public value, see Mark Moore, *Creating Public
      Value*.
37    Quoted in E Kelly and P Leyden (eds.) *What's Next: exploring the new terrain for
      business* (Cambridge MA: Perseus, 2002).
38    P Himanen, *The Hacker* (New York, NY: Random House, 2001).

# DEMOS – Licence to Publish

THE WORK (AS DEFINED BELOW) IS PROVIDED UNDER THE TERMS OF THIS LICENCE ("LICENCE"). THE WORK IS PROTECTED BY COPYRIGHT AND/OR OTHER APPLICABLE LAW. ANY USE OF THE WORK OTHER THAN AS AUTHORIZED UNDER THIS LICENCE IS PROHIBITED. BY EXERCISING ANY RIGHTS TO THE WORK PROVIDED HERE, YOU ACCEPT AND AGREE TO BE BOUND BY THE TERMS OF THIS LICENCE. DEMOS GRANTS YOU THE RIGHTS CONTAINED HERE IN CONSIDERATION OF YOUR ACCEPTANCE OF SUCH TERMS AND CONDITIONS.

1.  **Definitions**
    a   **"Collective Work"** means a work, such as a periodical issue, anthology or encyclopedia, in which the Work in its entirety in unmodified form, along with a number of other contributions, constituting separate and independent works in themselves, are assembled into a collective whole. A work that constitutes a Collective Work will not be considered a Derivative Work (as defined below) for the purposes of this Licence.
    b   **"Derivative Work"** means a work based upon the Work or upon the Work and other pre-existing works, such as a musical arrangement, dramatization, fictionalization, motion picture version, sound recording, art reproduction, abridgment, condensation, or any other form in which the Work may be recast, transformed, or adapted, except that a work that constitutes a Collective Work or a translation from English into another language will not be considered a Derivative Work for the purpose of this Licence.
    c   **"Licensor"** means the individual or entity that offers the Work under the terms of this Licence.
    d   **"Original Author"** means the individual or entity who created the Work.
    e   **"Work"** means the copyrightable work of authorship offered under the terms of this Licence.
    f   **"You"** means an individual or entity exercising rights under this Licence who has not previously violated the terms of this Licence with respect to the Work, or who has received express permission from DEMOS to exercise rights under this Licence despite a previous violation.
2.  **Fair Use Rights.** Nothing in this licence is intended to reduce, limit, or restrict any rights arising from fair use, first sale or other limitations on the exclusive rights of the copyright owner under copyright law or other applicable laws.
3.  **Licence Grant.** Subject to the terms and conditions of this Licence, Licensor hereby grants You a worldwide, royalty-free, non-exclusive, perpetual (for the duration of the applicable copyright) licence to exercise the rights in the Work as stated below:
    a   to reproduce the Work, to incorporate the Work into one or more Collective Works, and to reproduce the Work as incorporated in the Collective Works;
    b   to distribute copies or phonorecords of, display publicly, perform publicly, and perform publicly by means of a digital audio transmission the Work including as incorporated in Collective Works. The above rights may be exercised in all media and formats whether now known or hereafter devised. The above rights include the right to make such modifications as are technically necessary to exercise the rights in other media and formats. All rights not expressly granted by Licensor are hereby reserved.
4.  **Restrictions.** The licence granted in Section 3 above is expressly made subject to and limited by the following restrictions:
    a   You may distribute, publicly display, publicly perform, or publicly digitally perform the Work only under the terms of this Licence, and You must include a copy of, or the Uniform Resource Identifier for, this Licence with every copy or phonorecord of the Work You distribute, publicly display, publicly perform, or publicly digitally perform. You may not offer or impose any terms on the Work that alter or restrict the terms of this Licence or the recipients' exercise of the rights granted hereunder. You may not sublicence the Work. You must keep intact all notices that refer to this Licence and to the disclaimer of warranties. You may not distribute, publicly display, publicly perform, or publicly digitally perform the Work with any technological measures that control access or use of the Work in a manner inconsistent with the terms of this Licence Agreement. The above applies to the Work as incorporated in a Collective Work, but this does not require the Collective Work apart from the Work itself to be made subject to the terms of this Licence. If You create a Collective Work, upon notice from any Licensor You must, to the extent practicable, remove from the Collective Work any reference to such Licensor or the Original Author, as requested.
    b   You may not exercise any of the rights granted to You in Section 3 above in any manner that is primarily intended for or directed toward commercial advantage or private monetary

compensation. The exchange of the Work for other copyrighted works by means of digital file-sharing or otherwise shall not be considered to be intended for or directed toward commercial advantage or private monetary compensation, provided there is no payment of any monetary compensation in connection with the exchange of copyrighted works.

**c**   If you distribute, publicly display, publicly perform, or publicly digitally perform the Work or any Collective Works, You must keep intact all copyright notices for the Work and give the Original Author credit reasonable to the medium or means You are utilizing by conveying the name (or pseudonym if applicable) of the Original Author if supplied; the title of the Work if supplied. Such credit may be implemented in any reasonable manner; provided, however, that in the case of a Collective Work, at a minimum such credit will appear where any other comparable authorship credit appears and in a manner at least as prominent as such other comparable authorship credit.

**5. Representations, Warranties and Disclaimer**

**a**   By offering the Work for public release under this Licence, Licensor represents and warrants that, to the best of Licensor's knowledge after reasonable inquiry:

**i**   Licensor has secured all rights in the Work necessary to grant the licence rights hereunder and to permit the lawful exercise of the rights granted hereunder without You having any obligation to pay any royalties, compulsory licence fees, residuals or any other payments;

**ii**   The Work does not infringe the copyright, trademark, publicity rights, common law rights or any other right of any third party or constitute defamation, invasion of privacy or other tortious injury to any third party.

**b**   EXCEPT AS EXPRESSLY STATED IN THIS LICENCE OR OTHERWISE AGREED IN WRITING OR REQUIRED BY APPLICABLE LAW, THE WORK IS LICENSED ON AN "AS IS" BASIS, WITHOUT WARRANTIES OF ANY KIND, EITHER EXPRESS OR IMPLIED INCLUDING, WITHOUT LIMITATION, ANY WARRANTIES REGARDING THE CONTENTS OR ACCURACY OF THE WORK.

**6. Limitation on Liability.** EXCEPT TO THE EXTENT REQUIRED BY APPLICABLE LAW, AND EXCEPT FOR DAMAGES ARISING FROM LIABILITY TO A THIRD PARTY RESULTING FROM BREACH OF THE WARRANTIES IN SECTION 5, IN NO EVENT WILL LICENSOR BE LIABLE TO YOU ON ANY LEGAL THEORY FOR ANY SPECIAL, INCIDENTAL, CONSEQUENTIAL, PUNITIVE OR EXEMPLARY DAMAGES ARISING OUT OF THIS LICENCE OR THE USE OF THE WORK, EVEN IF LICENSOR HAS BEEN ADVISED OF THE POSSIBILITY OF SUCH DAMAGES.

**7. Termination**

**a**   This Licence and the rights granted hereunder will terminate automatically upon any breach by You of the terms of this Licence. Individuals or entities who have received Collective Works from You under this Licence, however, will not have their licences terminated provided such individuals or entities remain in full compliance with those licences. Sections 1, 2, 5, 6, 7, and 8 will survive any termination of this Licence.

**b**   Subject to the above terms and conditions, the licence granted here is perpetual (for the duration of the applicable copyright in the Work). Notwithstanding the above, Licensor reserves the right to release the Work under different licence terms or to stop distributing the Work at any time; provided, however that any such election will not serve to withdraw this Licence (or any other licence that has been, or is required to be, granted under the terms of this Licence), and this Licence will continue in full force and effect unless terminated as stated above.

**8. Miscellaneous**

**a**   Each time You distribute or publicly digitally perform the Work or a Collective Work, DEMOS offers to the recipient a licence to the Work on the same terms and conditions as the licence granted to You under this Licence.

**b**   If any provision of this Licence is invalid or unenforceable under applicable law, it shall not affect the validity or enforceability of the remainder of the terms of this Licence, and without further action by the parties to this agreement, such provision shall be reformed to the minimum extent necessary to make such provision valid and enforceable.

**c**   No term or provision of this Licence shall be deemed waived and no breach consented to unless such waiver or consent shall be in writing and signed by the party to be charged with such waiver or consent.

**d**   This Licence constitutes the entire agreement between the parties with respect to the Work licensed here. There are no understandings, agreements or representations with respect to the Work not specified here. Licensor shall not be bound by any additional provisions that may appear in any communication from You. This Licence may not be modified without the mutual written agreement of DEMOS and You.